THE AMERICAN COMPOSERS SERIES

Samuel Barber: Complete Piano Music

Ed. 3453

G. SCHIRMER, Inc.

DISTRIBUTED BY

HAL•LEONARD®
CORPORATION
7777 W. BLUEMOUND RD. P.O. BOX 13819 MILWAUKEE, WI 53213

SAMUEL BARBER: A PERSONAL NOTE

I had the good fortune and privilege to be Samuel Barber's editor and friend for many years. The sailing was not always smooth but it was never really rough. He demanded very little—only intelligence and perfection.

Always elegantly dressed and urbane in manner and speech, he seemed to belong to the world of Henry James and Edith Wharton. But not quite: his conversation was sprinkled with ribaldry, his graffiti humor and wry stories (Sam was a malicious raconteur) always phrased in a lapidary style.

But beneath the aristocratic surface of his cosmopolitan gaiety lived a most private, dedicated, and disciplined man. His wit was a line of defense against a deep-rooted melancholia. This interplay between the two sides of his nature is apparent in his music; passion and resignation are inherent in everything he composed. He never wavered in his fidelity to the music he completely loved—that of Bach, Chopin, Fauré, among others. And even when he added contemporary techniques to his style, he never fully succumbed to any current fad. Whatever he found useful was applied so discreetly that his basic profile was in no way obscured. Detractors consider his refusal to plunge completely into the twentieth century a weakness; to his admirers, it was the source of his strength. In any case, it gives his genius its original stamp. For a time, in the early seventies, he was hurt because he thought he was being bypassed by the younger generation; he felt he was "a shadowy figure from another age." Unfortunately, he did not live long enough to smile at the headlong rush to tonality so evident today.

I do not mean to convey the impression that this meticulous musician was a cynical or lugubrious figure. He certainly was not. Like all of us, Barber had sacred and profane qualities in unequal measure. He was a fanatically loyal friend and a wonderfully unfair enemy. Of a composer who said his music belonged in a night club, he parried: "I wish it were true. I'd make a pile of dough, take a cruise around the world, and read Ibsen in Norwegian." When I thought I had finessed him by bringing to his attention that the fugue theme in his Piano Sonata had an affinity with a theme in *Porgy and Bess,* he trumped me by saying: "How clever of you. I wish I had thought of that myself." And I still chuckle at his trenchant remark about the Piano Sonata: "I would have made it harder if they had given me more money." (The piece was commissioned by the League of Composers with a paltry sum presented to the League by Irving Berlin and Richard Rodgers.)

On another occasion, when we had a meeting with a book publisher who wanted him to write his memoirs, Barber turned to me and said: "Why don't *you* write my autobiography? You have more imagination than I have." He treated his own music lightly. He often said he did not want the *Adagio for Strings* to be played at his funeral: "It is too banal a thing to do." Once, after a well-meant but overlong party given in his honor (his talent for being amused was limited), Sam, my wife, and I were waiting for a train at a suburban station. Suddenly he fell to his knee and sang in falsetto to my wife: "To the monument! Alexas, go tell him I have slain myself," from the final pages of *Antony and Cleopatra.* I do not know what the onlookers thought of this precipitate action, but I, knowing how deeply he had been wounded by the unwarranted failure of the opera's initial performance, was deeply moved.

These few vignettes serve to hide the seismographically sensitive person beneath his often theatrical pose. Barber's range of feeling and areas of knowledge were enormous, not only in music but in the field of general culture, particularly literature. He was at home in many languages. His favorite authors were Turgenev and Trollope. Not surprisingly, with his Pepysian propinquities, he was addicted to memoirs and diaries. At one of our last lunches (that included two of his favorite foods, asparagus with hollandaise sauce and chocolate ice cream), we savored the lustier anecdotes of Marchand's *Byron's Letters and Journals.*

Barber rarely discussed his own music (a modesty alien to most composers); if he did, he made sport of it, although he was ferociously proud of it. I always felt that he thought he never measured up to his own expectations or exacting standards. No one could. But what he gave us is so warmly human and finely tooled that he can be forgiven his own misgivings. The closest I ever got to the vital nerve center of his reticence was after he played me *Souvenirs.* At that time the piece had no name and I did not know its genealogy. (It was originally composed as a four-hand work to be performed by him and a close friend at parties.) When he finished, I said: "I don't want to insult you Sam (remembering the night-club music episode), but it reminds me of the Biltmore Hotel and F. Scott Fitzgerald." I got an exuberant hug. "That's it. But it isn't the Biltmore. It's the Palm Court at the Plaza."

It would not be difficult for me to expand these few reminiscences into a full-blown essay. But I think I have said enough to convey some slight sense of this extraordinary, civilized, and complex man. His music, of course, needs no introduction.

—PAUL WITTKE

This new edition of the Complete Piano Music has been expanded to include one unpublished work, *Interlude I.* In addition, some minor corrections (which were brought to our attention by John Browning) have been made to the music. Mr. Browning has recorded the Complete Piano Music on Music Masters (CD-67122-2), which won the 1994 Grammy Award.

CONTENTS

Excursions

I

Samuel Barber, Op. 20

II

In slow blues tempo ♩ = 60

III

IV

Tempo I°

Sonata for Piano

I

Samuel Barber, Op. 26

Tempo I°

II

Allegro vivace e leggero ♩. = 152

III

IV

Fuga

allargando il meno possibile

string. e cresc. poco a poco

to Charles Turner

Souvenirs

Samuel Barber, Op. 28
Arranged for piano solo
by the composer

I
Waltz

Un poco meno ♩. = 66

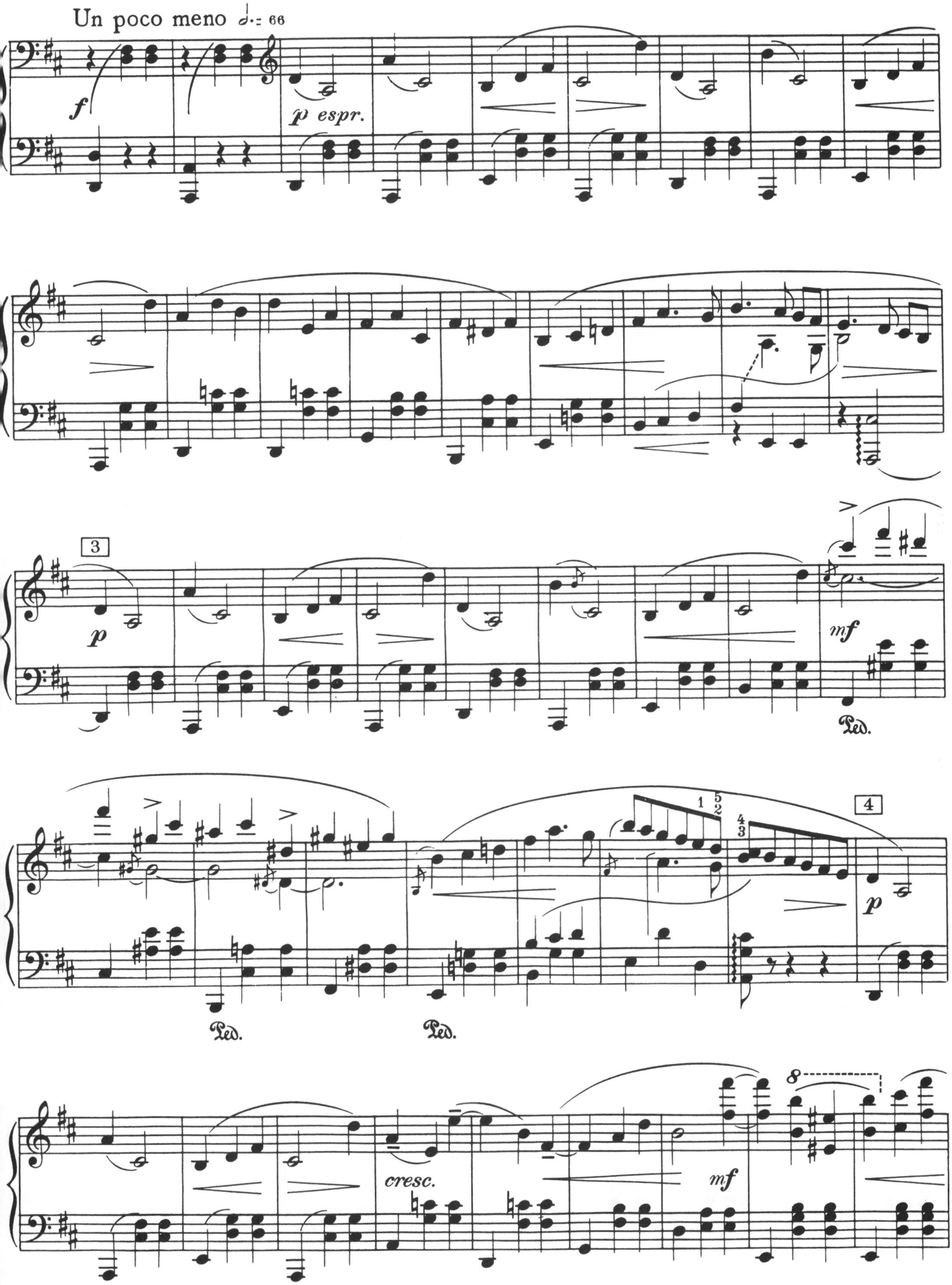

II
Schottische

Tempo di Schottische, allegro ma non troppo ♩ = 88

73

Doppio mosso, presto

2:30

III
Pas de deux

IV

Two-Step

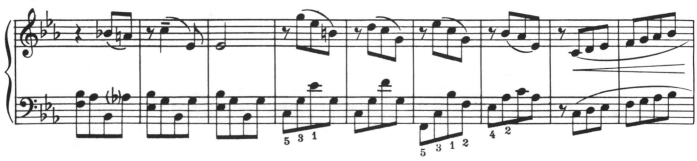

V
Hesitation-Tango

VI
Galop

Nocturne

(Homage to John Field)

Samuel Barber, Op. 33

Ballade

Samuel Barber, Op. 46

For Jeanne

Interlude I

Samuel Barber, Op. Post.
(1931)

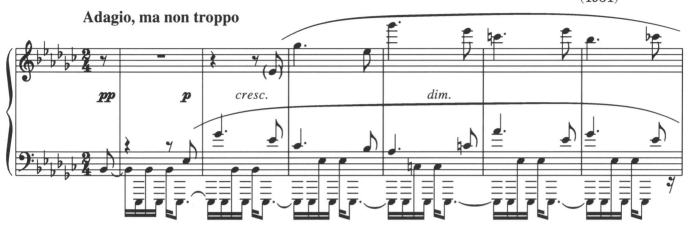

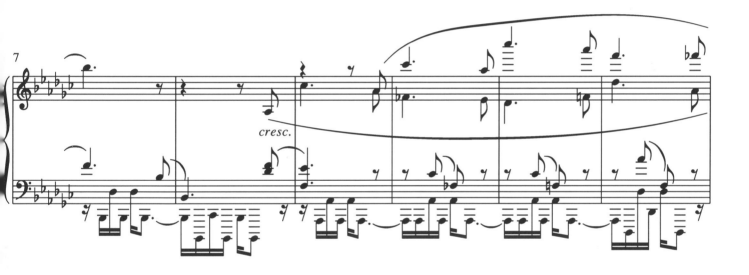

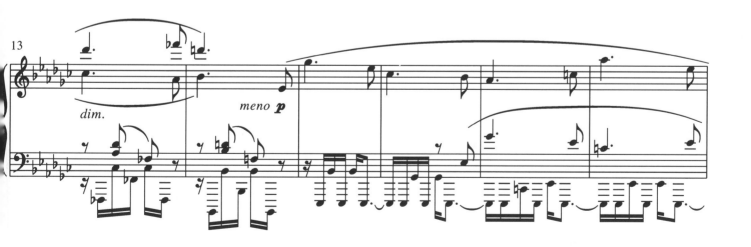

Meno mosso

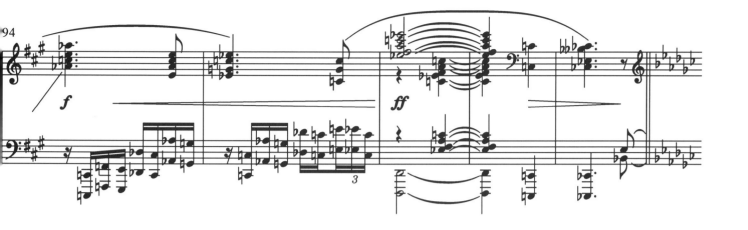

Tempo I

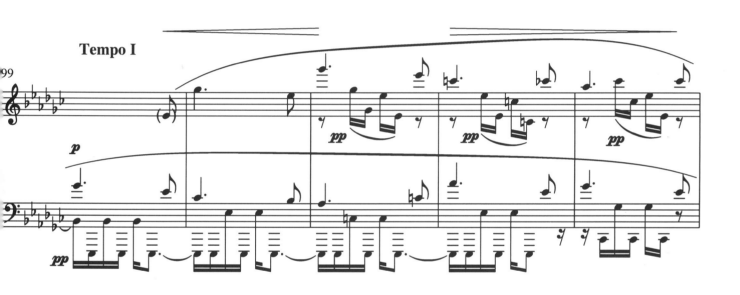

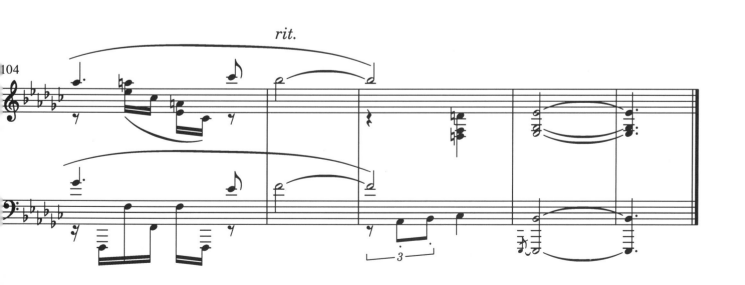